How Did the Creature Cross the Road?

by Joanne Mattern

RED
CHAIR
·PRESS·

Egremont, Massachusetts

RED CHAIR PRESS
BOOKS FOR YOUNG READERS

Wildlife Rescue is produced and published by Red Chair Press:

Red Chair Press LLC   PO Box 333   South Egremont, MA 01258-0333

www.redchairpress.com

Publisher's Cataloging-In-Publication Data
Names: Mattern, Joanne, 1963- author.
Title: How did the creature cross the road? / by Joanne Mattern.

Description: South Egremont, MA : Red Chair Press, [2022] | Series:
    Wildlife rescue | Interest age level: 007-010. | Includes index and
    suggested resources for further reading. | Summary: "Roadway overpasses
    in Canada's Banff National Park allow bears and deer to safely cross
    roads, Readers also discover fish ladders and 'salmon cannons' in the
    U.S. Pacific Northwest, rope swings for monkeys in China, and colorful
    crab bridges in Australia"--Provided by publisher.

Identifiers: ISBN 9781643711911 (hardcover) | ISBN 9781643711959
    (softcover) | ISBN 9781643711997 (ePDF) | ISBN 9781643712031 (ePub 3
    S&L) | ISBN 9781643712079 (ePub 3 TR) | ISBN 9781643712116 (Kindle)

Subjects: LCSH: Wildlife crossings--Juvenile literature. | Fishways--
    Juvenile literature. | Wildlife habitat improvement--Juvenile
    literature. | Animals and civilization--Juvenile literature. |
    Mammals--Conservation--Juvenile literature. | Fishes--Conservation--
    Juvenile literature. | CYAC: Wildlife habitat improvement. | Animals
    and civilization. | Mammals. | Fishes.

Classification: LCC SK356.W54 M384 2022 (print) | LCC SK356.W54 (ebook) |
    DDC 333.95/416--dc23

LC record available at: https://lccn.loc.gov/2021945553

Copyright © 2023 Red Chair Press LLC

RED CHAIR PRESS, the RED CHAIR and associated logos are registered
trademarks of Red Chair Press LLC.

All rights reserved. No part of this book may be reproduced, stored in an
information or retrieval system, or transmitted in any form by any means,
electronic, mechanical including photocopying, recording, or otherwise
without the prior written permission from the Publisher. For permissions,
contact info@redchairpress.com

Photo credits: Cover, p. 1, 4, 5, 7–10, 13, 18, 22, 23, 27: iStock; p. 6, 11, 16, 20, 26, 28, back
cover: Shutterstock; p. 14–15: Courtesy of Parks Canada; p. .24–25: Courtesy of Whooshh
Innovations; p. 12: ©Joel Sartore; p. 17: ©AP Images; p. 19: ©Caters News; p. 21: ©Yvonne
McKenzie/ Wondrous World Images 2021

Printed in United States of America
0422 1P CGF22

Table of Contents

Danger on the Road

Highways are dangerous places. Cars and trucks zoom by almost all the time. It's very hard to cross a highway safely.

Most people know better than to cross a highway, especially if cars and trucks are coming. But animals cross roads all the time. When they do, bad things can happen.

As more and more highways are built, more animals get into trouble. Animals cross highways to find food or escape a **predator**. They may cross to find other animals to mate with. Highways are often built in the middle of an animal's **territory**. The creatures don't know they shouldn't cross. Sometimes people have to help them.

Canada's Animal Crossings

In 1996, Parks Canada took on a big project. This group knew that thousands of elk, moose, bear, and wolves were killed every year crossing highways in Canada's national parks. People were also hurt or killed in these accidents. Parks Canada came up with an unusual answer to this problem.

Mountain goats stopping traffic on a busy highway.

Parks Canada knew many of its roads are built
where animals cross to find food or water.

FAST FACTS:
Banff National Park was the first National Park in Canada in 1885. And in 1911, Canada was the first country in the world to create a national parks service.

Parks Canada built fences along 55 miles of highway in Banff National Park. The fences would keep animals off the road. But they still needed a way to cross. So Parks Canada built bridges for them!

At first, people laughed at the idea of animal bridges. They thought the project was a waste of money. However, the project was a big success. Canada even built more crossings in other areas of the country.

Over and Under

Today, there are six **overpasses** in the park. Elk and deer started using these bridges even before they were finished. These big animals safely crossed the road without getting in cars' way.

Grizzly bears and wolves use the overpasses too. Scientists placed cameras along the trail. They found more than 200,000 animals have used the overpasses.

A moose uses a wildlife overpass to safely
cross a highway in Banff National Park.

Not all animals like being out in the open on a high bridge. So Parks Canada also built 38 **underpasses** and tunnels. Cougars and black bears use these tunnels. They cross safely under the highway while cars and trucks whiz by over their heads.

Security cameras took images of some
of the animals using the tunnels.

Elephants Exit Here!

In 2011, the first elephant underpass was opened near the slopes of Mt. Kenya. Construction of roads, housing and shops had cut off the natural pathway between the two elephant **habitats**. Rescuers say the tunnel allows the elephants to move safely between their homes now.

Africa's first elephant underpass opened in 2011 near Mt. Kenya.

Crab Crossing

Mammals aren't the only animals who have trouble crossing the road. Crabs do too! Every year, millions of red crabs cross roads on Christmas Island in Australia. These crabs **migrate** to the ocean to mate and lay eggs. Sadly, many are hit by cars.

Rangers at Christmas Island National Park decided to take action. They built 31 underpasses. These tunnels allow crabs to cross the roads safely.

Millions of red crabs use the tunnels.

There was one place where a tunnel could not be built. So, the rangers built a bridge instead! The bridge is 16 feet (5 m) high. It is covered with a metal web. Crabs climb up and down this tall bridge while cars travel safely underneath.

People come from all over the world to watch the Christmas Island crab migration. Many of them come to see the crab bridge too!

Fish Ladders and Cannons

Fish don't have to worry about getting hit by cars on the road. But they still have a hard time getting where they need to go. Salmon migrate up rivers in the northwestern United States. However, dams sometimes block their way.

People build fish ladders to help fish. These aren't real ladders. Instead, they are a series of small pools. Each pool is a little higher than the one before it. The fish can jump from one pool to the next to get up and over the dam.

Salmon jumping up the ladders.

The cannon is soft and gentle for the fish.

Fish ladders are helpful, but sometimes salmon need a faster way to travel. In 2014, a Native American tribe in Washington state wanted to reintroduce salmon to the Columbia River. However, there was a big dam in the way. A fish ladder just wouldn't work. Then a man named Vincent Bryan invented the salmon cannon.

The salmon cannon is a long, soft tube. It shoots each salmon over the dam in just a few seconds. The salmon aren't hurt. The quick cannon shot helps them save their energy. That means the fish have a better chance of swimming to their new home.

Creature Crossings

As people build more roads in animal habitats, creatures need help to stay alive. Bridges, tunnels, and cannons are just a few of the ways people have stepped up to help our animal neighbors.

Glossary

habitat: a place or environment where an animal or plant naturally lives and grows

mammals: a class of animals who are warm-blooded, with hair, and give birth to live babies (not as unhatched eggs)

migrate: to travel from one area to another

overpasses: roads that pass over another road

predator: an animal that hunts other animals for food

rangers: people who work in a forest or park

territory: land where animals live

underpasses: roads that pass under another road

Learn More in the Library

Bailey, Linda. *Carson Crosses Canada*. Tundra Books, 2017.

Blewett, Ashlee. *Mission: Elephant Rescue*. National Geographic Kids, 2014.

Godkin, Celia. *The Wolves Return*. Pajama Press, 2017.

Rae, Rowena. *Salmon: Swimming for Survival*. Orca Books, 2022.

Index

About the Author

Joanne Mattern is the author of many books for children including the Core Content: ***Earth's Amazing Animals Series***. She loves writing about sports, all kinds of animals, and interesting people. Mattern lives in New York State with her family.

MW01166373